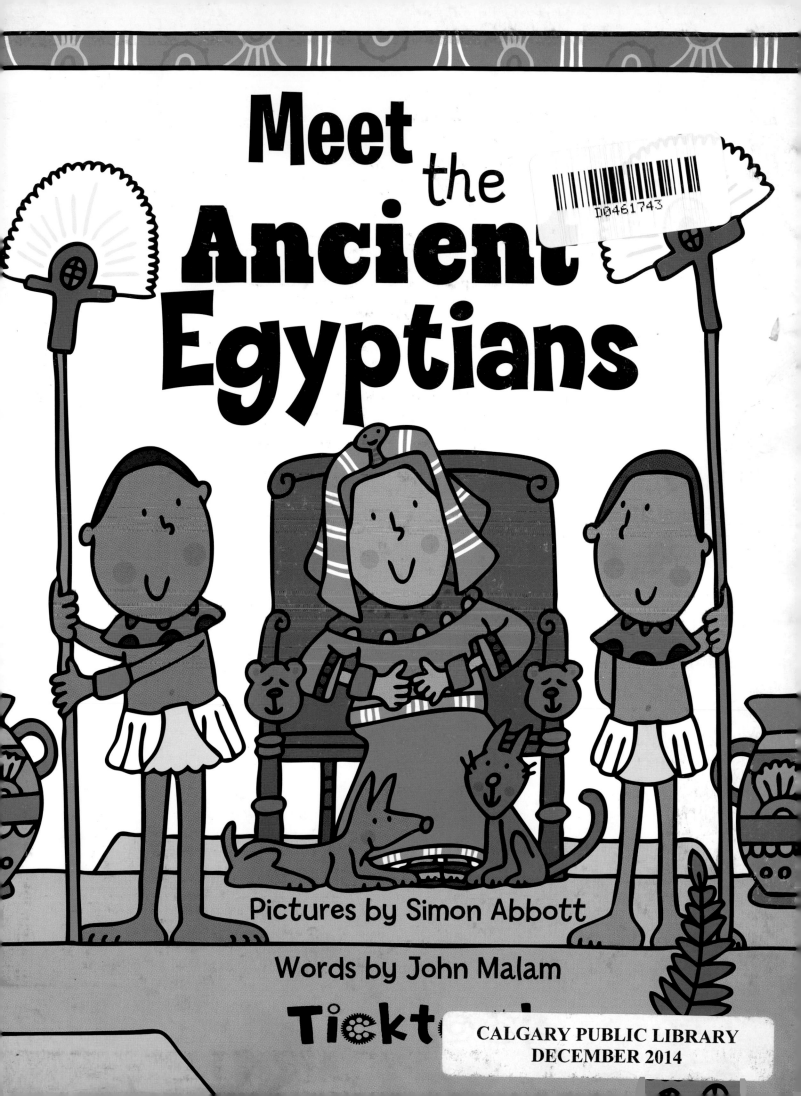

Meet the Ancient Egyptians

Pictures by Simon Abbott

Words by John Malam

Ticktock

Enter Ancient Egypt...

Ancient Egypt was a strange and amazing place. It was not at all like the world today. It was a land of pyramids, mummies, and powerful rulers.

ASIA

AFRICA

ANCIENT EGYPT

I'm stuck in the mud!

Ancient Egypt was a very long, thin strip of farmland in northeast Africa. It lay on either side of the mighty River Nile, and, although hundreds of miles long, it was only about **six miles wide**.

The people who lived along this strip of land called it the **"Black Land,"** because the soil was black and muddy.

Most ordinary people were **farmers**. They worked hard, and the food they produced fed everyone – from the poorest person to the poshest pharaoh.

Grrrrrr!

Perfect!

Ancient Egypt was ruled by powerful people called **pharaohs** (say fair-oh). Giant pyramids were built as their tombs, and their bodies were **mummified** to stop them rotting away.

Amazing Rulers

Ancient Egypt was ruled by a powerful king called a pharaoh. Some pharaohs ruled Egypt for many years.

Like kings and queens today, the pharaoh wore a **crown**. It showed he was the ruler of all Egypt. It wasn't a normal crown, but two made into one! It was called the **Double Crown**.

The pharaoh sometimes wore a **striped cloth** on his head, which came down to his shoulders. This wasn't to stop him from getting sunburned – it was to tell everyone he was in charge!

FUN FACTS

People worshipped and obeyed the pharaoh, because they believed he was a **god** in human form.

There were some women pharaohs, too. One was **Queen Hatshepsut**, who is shown in pictures with a fake beard!

THINGS TO DO

RELIGION ✓

GOVERNMENT ✓

ARMY ✓

LAW ✓

The pharaoh had lots to do. He was the leader of the **army**.
He was also the **chief priest**, which meant he was in charge of religion.
He was the leader of the **government** and made all the **laws**.

The pharaoh was allowed to have lots of wives!
A pharaoh's chief wife was called the **Great Royal Wife**.

Can I be the pharaoh next?

BOO!

Tutankhamun was just a boy when he became pharaoh – he was only nine or ten years old.

A pharaoh called **Ramesses II** had more than 100 children!

WOW!

An Awesome Army

The pharaoh had an army of soldiers to fight his enemies. But sometimes the pharaoh fought in battles himself, to show his people what a strong leader he was.

Eventually, ancient Egyptians needed a different type of army to defend themselves. So an army of about **20,000** soldiers was set up to serve all year round.

At first, the pharaoh's army was made up of **farmer-soldiers**. When they weren't working as soldiers, they were farmers. If the pharaoh needed them in battle, they had to leave their farms behind.

Reporting for duty, sir!

I'll be back soon, Daisy!

Soldiers wore **short kilts** but nothing on their chests and no shoes on their feet! A lucky few wore **leather helmets**.

Hey!

FUN FACTS

A brave warrior was given a **gold pendant** in the shape of a fly or a bee – just as soldiers are given medals today.

A bow could fire an arrow as far as **570 feet (175 meters)** – about the length of one and a half soccer fields!

Soldiers fought with bows and arrows, spears, swords, and axes. They carried **long shields** to protect their bodies.

Ready for action!

It's a draw!

6   6

Pharaohs liked to boast about the battles they won. The pharaoh **Ramesses II** claimed he had won a great battle at the city of **Kadesh**. Or had he? The leader of the other side also said he won.

Ooops!

Some soldiers were carried in **chariots**, pulled by two horses. One man steered the horses, and the other man fired arrows or threw spears.

A **chariot's** top speed was about 25 miles per hour - as fast as a charging elephant!

WOW!

Where's My Mummy?

The ancient Egyptians believed that a dead person came back to life in heaven, but they needed a body to come back to! So they created mummies - only the rich could afford them!

1. Mummy-makers collected the body and took it to the **desert**.

LUNGS

LIVER

INTESTINES

STOMACH

BRAIN BIN

2. Mummy-makers began by taking out the **lungs**, **intestines**, **liver**, and **stomach** and putting them into jars.

3. The **brain** came out, too, but it was thrown away.

4. The ancient Egyptians believed the **heart** controlled the body, so it was left inside.

NATRON

5. The body was covered with special salt, called **natron** (say nay-tron), to dry it out.

It took **15** days to clean the body out, **40** days to dry it, and **15** days to wrap it!

980 feet (300 meters) of linen were used to wrap a mummy - that's the length of **three** soccer fields!

6. When the body was dry, it was made to look real again. The **empty tummy** was filled with rags. Then false eyes and a wig were added!

7. Mummy-makers wrapped the body from head to toe with strips of linen. They placed **charms** between the layers to protect the person.

8. The mummy was put into a **wooden coffin**. Then the mummy was buried inside a tomb.

9. The mummy was buried with jewelry, food, and even musical instruments for the dead person to use in the afterlife.

Eyes were painted on the coffin – so the mummy inside could see outside!

Cats, dogs, birds, fish, and even crocodiles were also made into mummies!

Poor old Tigger!

WOW!

Perfect Pyramids

Dead pharaohs were buried in special tombs. The first pharaohs were buried inside amazing tombs called pyramids. Altogether, there are about 120 pyramids!

The most famous **pyramids** (say pir-ra-mids) are at Giza. There are three massive pyramids built for pharaohs, and some smaller ones built for their wives.

The Great Pyramid at Giza was built for the pharaoh **Khufu** (say koo-foo). It is the largest pyramid ever built. It took over 20 years to build, and work began while Khufu was still alive.

Keep up the good work!

Near the Giza pyramids is the **Sphinx** (say sfi-nks). This strange creature has the body of a lion and the head of a human. It was carved from a giant mound of rock.

Khufu's **mummified** body was buried in a secret room inside his pyramid. He was surrounded by things for him to use in heaven. But **tomb robbers** broke in and stole everything!

AIRSHAFT

KING'S CHAMBER

GRAND GALLERY

ENTRANCE

QUEEN'S CHAMBER

FALSE TOMB

1,999,998...
1,999,999...
2,000,000!

The Great Pyramid is made from more than **two million** blocks of stone. When it was finished, it was over 460 feet (140 meters) tall - that's about the same as ten houses on top of each other!

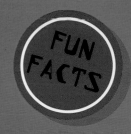
Pyramid builders didn't get it right at first! The first pyramid was the **Step Pyramid**, with six platforms.

Then they built the **Bent Pyramid**. The builders got it wrong, and halfway up they changed its shape.

Finally, they learned to make a **true pyramid**, with four smooth sides that came together in a point at the top.

Yippee!

Great Gods!

The ancient Egyptians believed in lots of gods - as many as 2,000. They thought the gods were in charge of the world and controlled everything in it.

Osiris was the god of farming and the god of the dead. Ancient Egyptians believed he was the first pharaoh - and so he also became the first ever mummy.

Amun-Ra was the sun god and king of all the gods. The ancient Egyptians believed he created the world.

The goddess **Isis** was married to Osiris. She was the goddess of nature and women, and one of the most loved goddesses of ancient Egypt.

When the wind blew, people thought it was the breath of **Amun-Ra**.

Eeew!

The River Nile was said to flow from the sweat of **Sobek**, the crocodile god.

Thoth was the cleverest god. He was in charge of wisdom, reading, writing, mathematics, and magic. He had the head of an ibis – a bird that lived along the River Nile.

Every day, **priests** washed special statues of the gods, dressed them in clean clothes, and left gifts of food. This was done to please the gods. In return, the gods protected the people.

Whoops! Missed a bit!

Horus was the son of Osiris and Isis. He was the sky god and was in charge of keeping law and order. He is shown in pictures with the head of a falcon.

The god **Seth** was so strong he carried a scepter that weighed 4,400 pounds (2,000 kilograms) - about as heavy as a small car!

The statues of the gods were housed in **temples**. People believed the god lived in the statue.

WOW!

Home Sweet Home

Most ancient Egyptians lived in villages scattered along the banks of the River Nile.

Families would often have at least five children! Houses might be **crowded** with grandparents, parents, and children all living together.

The **mothers** and **daughters** worked hard, cooking, cleaning, and making clothes for the family.

Fathers and **sons** went out to work, often as farmers. A father taught his sons how to do his job, so that one day they could work for themselves.

Young children had their hair **shaved off**, except for a long curl on one side.

Ancient Egyptian children loved **games** especially leapfrog and tug-of-war!

Houses were joined together in groups. The family ate and relaxed on the ground floor and used an open courtyard outside as a kitchen. At bedtime, the family climbed up steps onto the flat roof and slept in the open air.

Wake up, sleepyhead!

Morning, grandpop!

Houses were built from **bricks** made out of mud from the River Nile mixed with chopped straw. The sun baked the mud to make the bricks hard.

Food was cooked in the open air. People ate lots of bread, fruit, and vegetables, including dates, figs, onions, and beans.

People bit into **raw onions** the same way we eat apples - they probably had "onion breath!"

Girls got **married** when they were just 12 or 13 years old and boys when they were 14 or 15.

WOW!

The Mighty River Nile

The River Nile was incredibly important to the ancient Egyptians. It gave them fresh water to drink, to wash in, to give to their animals, and to water their crops.

The **River Nile** was ancient Egypt's busy "main road." Big cargo boats carried people, animals, and goods from place to place, while little boats were used to catch fish.

Once a year, the River Nile burst its banks and **flooded** the land. People wanted the river to flood because it washed a thick layer of black mud over farmers' fields, perfect for growing crops.

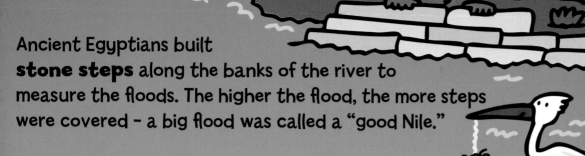

Ancient Egyptians built **stone steps** along the banks of the river to measure the floods. The higher the flood, the more steps were covered – a big flood was called a "good Nile."

Dangerous **crocodiles** and **hippopotamuses** lived in the River Nile!

Yikes!

Better get a moo-ve on!

Farmers scattered **seeds** by hand, then cattle trod them into the soil – before birds could eat them!

The **flood season** started in June and lasted until September. The River Nile flooded and spread out across the land.

The **growing season** was from October to January. Farmers divided the land into little fields and dug ditches from the fields to the river to water their crops.

February to May was the **harvest season**, when farmers gathered their crops.

Work, Work, Work

The ancient Egyptians were very busy people and there was always lots of work for them to do...

Most men worked as **farmers**, growing crops to feed the people and animals. Farmers were respected people because of the important work they did to feed everyone.

Special offer on the onions today!

A few men could read, write, and count. They were known as **scribes**. They wrote using signs known as **hieroglyphs** (say high-ro-gliff). There were more than 700 different hieroglyphs!

I always forget this one!

FUN FACTS

Scribes made paper from **papyrus reeds** that grew along the River Nile. Reeds were also made into paintbrushes.

Builders were easy to spot - they often walked bent over after carrying heavy stones for years.

Women worked as **dancers**. They danced to please the pharaoh at festivals. They ran and jumped, and did cartwheels, handstands, and backbends.

Weee-eee!

Some men worked in teams as **artists**. One man made a rough drawing and another colored it in.

Whenever there was a celebration, there was music. **Musicians** were usually women. They made music with pipes, drums, tambourines, bells, and cymbals. Music was thought to please the gods.

If they were bored and wanted some fun, **fishermen** pushed each other into the River Nile!

Ancient Egyptian Facts

Both men and women wore **makeup**. Eye paint was usually green or black and protected people's eyes from the bright sun.

The ancient Egyptians invented the **toothbrush**! It wasn't a brush like we use today but the twig of a tree. As it was chewed, it cleaned the teeth.

People still had **bad teeth**, though. This was because gritty sand got into their bread and wore their teeth away.

Sandy sandwich, anyone?

It took about **14 days** for a boat to sail along the length of the River Nile. The same journey took 45 days on land!

Trade you!

The ancient Egyptians did not use **money**. Instead, they bartered, or swapped things. A cow was worth 20 pigs!